First World War
and Army of Occupation
War Diary
France, Belgium and Germany

5 CAVALRY DIVISION
Divisional Troops
5 Field Squadron Royal Engineers
1 January 1917 - 20 April 1918

WO95/1163/3

The Naval & Military Press Ltd
www.nmarchive.com
Published in association with The National Archives

Published by

The Naval & Military Press Ltd

Unit 10 Ridgewood Industrial Park,

Uckfield, East Sussex,

TN22 5QE England

Tel: +44 (0) 1825 749494

www.naval-military-press.com

www.nmarchive.com

This diary has been reprinted in facsimile from the original. Any imperfections are inevitably reproduced and the quality may fall short of modern type and cartographic standards.

© **Crown Copyright**
Images reproduced by permission of The National Archives, London, England, 2015.

Contents

Document type	Place/Title	Date From	Date To
Heading	WO95/1163/3		
Heading	5 Cav Div Troops 5 Field SQ RE 1917 Jan-1918 Apr		
Heading	War Diary of 5th Field Squadron. R.E, From 1st January 1917 To 31st January 1917		
War Diary	Embreville	01/01/1917	23/02/1917
War Diary	Embreville (Abbcnlle 1/40000)	03/03/1917	29/03/1917
War Diary	Bois De Mereacourt	30/03/1917	30/03/1917
War Diary	Warfusee	31/03/1917	09/04/1917
War Diary	Rainecourt	10/04/1917	10/04/1917
War Diary	Tertry	12/04/1917	13/05/1917
War Diary	Montigny Dump	14/05/1917	09/07/1917
War Diary	Tertry	10/07/1917	13/07/1917
War Diary	Buire	14/07/1917	14/07/1917
War Diary	Suzanne	15/07/1917	15/07/1917
War Diary	Ribemont	16/07/1917	16/07/1917
War Diary	Marieux	17/07/1917	17/07/1917
War Diary	La Thieuloye	18/07/1917	19/07/1917
War Diary	Trois Vaux	20/07/1917	04/10/1917
War Diary	Watou	05/10/1917	15/10/1917
War Diary	Campagne	16/10/1917	17/10/1917
War Diary	Renty	17/10/1917	31/10/1917
Operation(al) Order(s)	Appendix A 5th Cavalry Division Operation Order No. 38	13/10/1917	13/10/1917
Miscellaneous	5th Cavalry Division March Table (Issued with Operation Order No. 38)		
Operation(al) Order(s)	Appendix "B" Canadian Cavalry Brigade Operation Order No. 43	15/10/1917	15/10/1917
Miscellaneous	Canadian Cavalry Division		
War Diary	Renty	02/11/1917	08/11/1917
War Diary	Labiez	09/11/1917	09/11/1917
War Diary	Remaisnil	10/11/1917	10/11/1917
War Diary	La Hussoye	11/11/1917	11/11/1917
War Diary	Cappy	12/11/1917	12/11/1917
War Diary	Bias Wood	13/11/1917	23/11/1917
War Diary	Suzanne	24/11/1917	24/11/1917
War Diary	Vaux	25/11/1917	27/11/1917
War Diary	Trefcon	28/11/1917	30/11/1917
War Diary	Jacquenne Copse	01/12/1917	02/12/1917
War Diary	Heudicourt	03/12/1917	05/12/1917
War Diary	Villers Faucon	06/12/1917	06/12/1917
War Diary	Caulaincourt	11/12/1917	16/12/1917
War Diary	Trefcon	17/12/1917	30/12/1917
Miscellaneous	Appendix A		
Miscellaneous	A Form. Messages And Signals. Appendix B		
Miscellaneous	Appendix C	01/12/1917	01/12/1917
Miscellaneous	A Form. Messages And Signals. Appendix D		
Miscellaneous	A Form. Messages And Signals. Appendix E		
Miscellaneous	Appendix F C.R.E. Cav. Corps		
Miscellaneous	Messages And Signals. Appendix G		
Miscellaneous	Appendix H C.R.E. Cav. Corps	04/12/1917	04/12/1917

Miscellaneous	A Form. Messages And Signals. Appendix J		
Miscellaneous	A Form. Messages And Signals. Appendix K		
Miscellaneous	C Form. Messages And Signals. Appendix L		
Miscellaneous	A Form. Messages And Signals. Appendix M		
War Diary	Trefcon	02/01/1918	23/01/1918
War Diary	Jeancourt	26/01/1918	27/01/1918
Miscellaneous	Appendix A Car. Cav. Corps	17/01/1918	17/01/1918
Miscellaneous	Appendix B Car. Cav. Corps	25/01/1918	25/01/1918
War Diary	Jeancourt	01/02/1918	13/03/1918
Miscellaneous	Athies	15/03/1918	15/03/1918
War Diary	Buire	16/03/1918	20/03/1918
War Diary	Doingt	21/03/1918	21/03/1918
War Diary	Barleux	22/03/1918	22/03/1918
War Diary	Foucaucourt	23/03/1918	23/03/1918
War Diary	Caix	24/03/1918	24/03/1918
War Diary	Bayonvillers	25/03/1918	27/03/1918
War Diary	Boves	28/03/1918	29/03/1918
War Diary	Cambos Fm	30/03/1918	31/03/1918
Miscellaneous	Appendix "A"		
War Diary	Lamotte-Brebiere	01/04/1918	05/04/1918
War Diary	Ailly-Le-Haut-Clocher	09/04/1918	09/04/1918
War Diary	Rouen	16/04/1918	20/04/1918
Miscellaneous	3rd Echelon Base	22/04/1918	22/04/1918

WO 95/1163/3

5 CAV DIV TROOPS

5 FIELD SQ. RE

1917 JAN – 1918 APR

SERIAL NO. 12

Confidential
War Diary
of

5th FIELD SQUADRON, R.E.

FROM 1st January 1917 TO 31st January 1917.

Army Form C. 2118.

WAR DIARY
or
INTELLIGENCE SUMMARY.
(Erase heading not required.)

6th Field Squadron RE
5th Cav Div
Vol. 25. Jan. 1917.

Instructions regarding War Diaries and Intelligence Summaries are contained in F.S. Regs., Part II. and the Staff Manual respectively. Title pages will be prepared in manuscript.

Place	Date	Hour	Summary of Events and Information	Remarks and references to Appendices
EMBREVILLE	1.1.17		In billets Embreville — Canadian 7th Troop absorbed into 5th & 7th Squadron on 1.1.17. 2nd Lt Jones & 10 Sappers proceed to join 1st & 2nd PIONEER Bat on 31.1.17 to relieve 2nd Lt CHANCE. 'A' Troop under Lt Guckhead commenced troop training	24
"	7.1.17		A Troop commence Third in/Litrup training. Pioneer course in Demolitions & bridging with offs & NCOs of Ambala Bde.	16
"			Major Callin to come as O.C. PARCO of P.(iv) 17.1.17. Class 11-18	16
"	14.1.17		'B' Troop commence Troop training. Pioneer course for offs & NCOs of 2nd Bde.	16
"	18.1.17		Capt Daley & Lieut Sadlier ATTRE, 1st Army Bridging school training R.E. 2175 Roys	5
			On 30-1.17	
"	21.1.17		'B' Troop commence 3rd course Bomb Progress & Classes of Bde schemes	
"	23.1.17		" Pioneer course for offs & NCOs & cases	
"			Any have first interfacer with army school	
"	31.1.17		HQrs of Squadron engaged in preparing sketches & reports on roads & the Bush Area	16

F.J. Colquin
Major
O.C. 5/70 Squadron RE

WAR DIARY or INTELLIGENCE SUMMARY.

Army Form C. 2118.

5th Cadet Squadron RFC
1st Can. Div.?
Feb 25th 1917

Place	Date	Hour	Summary of Events and Information	Remarks and references to Appendices
Easeville 1917			In hut 15 Easeville Canadians & Troop Worked into 5 & 13 Squadron on 11/2/17	
			22th Lectures to Jeffrey Horsey & Jones Etching worked out 25/1/17 to relieve 2th Course	
	7.1.17		A Troop commenced Workshop Training. Pioneer Course in Erection & Repairing of	
			Both Off & NCOs of Ambala 13ac	W
			Major Elton to Course at ????	W
	10.1.17		"B" Troop commenced Troop Training. Pioneer Course for Off & NCOs 60 Squadron 13ac	W
	10.1.17		Capt Jersey lectures at AIRE 1st Army Brigade School transferred to 219 P Sqn	W
			Oct 31 — 1.17	
	20.1.17		"B" Troop commenced 2 week Troop Training Officers/Can Bde attend Schemes	
	22.1.17		" " 3rd " Pioneer Course for Ambala 1 & 60 "Bad Weather	
	25.1.17		My have first interview with wing school	
			Have 5 Squadrons engaged in ????? staffing repairs & exhibiting that UE in the Brit Area	

F L Collins
Major RE
OC 5th 70 Squadron RE

WAR DIARY or INTELLIGENCE SUMMARY.

(Erase heading not required.)

Army Form C. 2118.

5th Field Squadron R.E.
5th Cav. Divn.
Vol 26 Feb 1917

Place	Date	Hour	Summary of Events and Information	Remarks and references to Appendices
EMBREVILLE	1.2.17		At billets Embreville. B troop completes 3rd weeks training	H.C.
	1.2.17		Capt. T.A. FARQUHARSON I.A.R. joined from 4th Fd Sqdn RE	H.C.
	4.2.17		'B' Troop commenced 4th week troop training. Hard frost interferes with riding	H.C.
	12.2.17		C Troop " 1st week "	H.C.
	10.2.17		Lt Matheson & party reported unit for work with Can. Pioneer Battn	H.C.
	"		Lt Lees & 10 men proceed with 1st C'RAD Pioneer Battn to near DOULLENS	H.C.
	19.2.17		'C' Troop commenced 2nd week troop training. Major COLVIN R.E. & Divn'l School at AULT.	H.C.
	9.2.17		Bridging Detts 31 O.R. & 35 D.H. 13 R. Horses with boat equipment left Sqdn to form Cops Bridging Train.	H.C.
	23.2.17		'B' Troop under Lt Chance to Villets at HAUTEBUT in Cav. Lw. Bde Area for training in saps & in conjunction with Cav. Corps. Bde work on Horse Disp at FRIVILLE & on roads in Divnl area which were cut up by frost & thaw	H.C.

H. Colvin
Maj. R.E.
O.C. 5th Fd Sqdn R.E.

Army Form C. 2118.

WAR DIARY
or
INTELLIGENCE SUMMARY.
(Erase heading not required.)

"F" Fd Squadron
5- Can Div
Vol 27 March 1917

Instructions regarding War Diaries and Intelligence Summaries are contained in F.S. Regs., Part II. and the Staff Manual respectively. Title pages will be prepared in manuscript.

Place	Date	Hour	Summary of Events and Information	Remarks and references to Appendices
	3.17		C Troop under Lt Mathewson to billets at HAUTEBUT in Can. Cav Bde area for training on the Sands.	App
	13-3-17 to 18th		1 Section of the Corps Bridging Park arrived on the 13th, and Bridging was carried out daily by all Troops from VAUVILLERS	App
	20-3-17		The Squadron left Winter Billets and marched to BERNAPRÉ.	App
	21/3/17		The Div'l Engineers Parks at GAMACHES with 2 Lt Dinsmore Reinforcements joined to settle up this Area. Maj Colvin reassumed command.	App
	22/3/17		The Squadron continued the march East to PLUY.	App 3
	23/3/17		The Squadron continued the march East to CERISY.	App 3
	24/3/17		Lt Greathead with A Troop joined the AMBALA Bde; Lt Lee with B Troop joined the CANADIAN Cav. Bgde.	App 3
	25/3/17		C Troop & Hd Qrs joined the SECUNDERABAD Bgde. The advanced to bivouacs at the Bois de NERACOURT. Tool Carts /3 hours	App
	26/3/17		"B" Echelon joins the Div'l "B" Echelon at HERBÉCOURT. C Troop & Hd Qrs joins the AMBALA Bgde. The march to ESTRÉES-en-Chaussé for work on repair to damaged roads	App
	27/3/17		Capt Jagan R.A.M.C. rejoined the Squadron relieving Capt McLean transported to Mhow C.I.A.	App
	28/3/17		A & C Troops work on dressing mud craters at Estrées + TERTRY.	
	29/3/17		H.Q. & A Troop marches to billets in depots at BOIS DE NERÉAVOUCOURT. C Troop marches to join 5ec Bde Ade H/C in bivouac near CLÉRY	

EMBREVILLE (Abbeville 1/40,000)

A.M. Colvin Maj RE

Army Form C. 2118.

WAR DIARY
or
INTELLIGENCE SUMMARY.
(Erase heading not required.)

3rd 7th Sqdn
5th Cav. Dv. vol 27 March 1917

Place	Date	Hour	Summary of Events and Information	Remarks and references to Appendices
BOIS de MEREAUCOURT	30.3.17		H.Q. & A Troops marched with Ambala Cav Bde to billets in WARFUSEE ABANCOURT	
WARFUSEE	31.3.17		In billets. H.Q. + A Troop with Ambala Bde at WARFUSEE B Troop " " " at BAY ON VILLERS C Troop " " Canadian " at CAPPY. 'B' schln rejoined H.Q. During the operations from 23-3-17 to 28-3-17, Major Collin was attached to Divl. H.Q. at PERONNE and carried out reconnaissances of roads & bridges in forward area on the IVth Army front (Ambala Bde front from BEAUVOIS to ROISEL Can Bde front from ROISEL (excl.) to Equancourt & further), also carried out a reconnaissance for a defensive line in line BEAUVOIS - COULAINCOURT - POEUILLY - FLECHIN - BERNES - HAMELET - MARQUAIX - LONGAVESNES - NURLU (23°.24°.25°.) to be occupied by A + C Troops were employed with Can 1 Inft. working parties making burning mp craters in AMBALA Bde area, also the instrs for a bridge training at TERTRY were commenced, it was ascertained that all bridges had to take 8 tons with tank axle. B Troop remained with Can Cav Bde & reconnoitred the roads on 27th, went up with Bde to the attack on GUYENCOURT AVLUICOURT & entered the villages immediately after the capture. No battle casualties. T.I. Collin Major R.E.	

WAR DIARY

or

INTELLIGENCE SUMMARY

Army Form C. 2118.

Vol. 28

5th Md Sqdn RE
5th Can. Div. Vol. 28 April 1917

Place	Date	Hour	Summary of Events and Information	Remarks and references to Appendices
MARFUSÉE	1-4-17		H.Q. & A Troop with Ambala Bde at MARFUSÉE	
	↑		B " " Can Cav Bde " BAYONVILLERS	
			C Troop - SEC'BAD Cav Bde " CAPPY	
			Dismounted Bde's at HAMEL at work on dismantling Camps. Go Mens to FOUQUESCOURT	
			A & B Troop employed on improvements & billets for SEC'BAD Bde.	no 9-4-17
	9-4-17		Lt Jones & 12 Sappers left at Gommecourt to clear Rd & Rd. Stores from district area	H.
	↓			
RAINECOURT	10-4-17		All Troops rejoined H.Q. & squadron marched to billets in RAINECOURT	H.
			Lt Jones & Dismounted men at FOUCAUCOURT working on roads in III Corps area	H.
			Party on station to LIHONS - CHAULNES Rd to SEC'BAD Bde.	
TERTRY	12-4-17		marched to Ravine Camp in H.9.c.8.8 near TERTRY at 1.30 p.m. arrived in same time	H.
"	13-4-17		men in German stable, horses in the open	
"			Lt Jones & Dismounts Reinforcements reported "guard"	
"	14-4-17		Troops employed with their Bde's on repairing Huts Standings Shelters & Bivouacs	
	↑		200 men per Bde under RE. Superman employed on repair roads & filling	
			in craters in area ATHIES - CROIX MOLIGNEUX - TERTRY - TREFCON CAULAINCOURT	
	21-4-17		RE stores obtained from CE. IV Corps from NESLE - MIENCOURT - ROYE - PERONNE Rd & LAFRAYE	H.

F.M. Allan Major RE

Army Form C. 2118.

WAR DIARY
or
INTELLIGENCE SUMMARY.

(Erase heading not required.)

5th Field Squadron RE
5th Cav. Divn. [illegible] April 1917

Place	Date	Hour	Summary of Events and Information	Remarks and references to Appendices
	22-4-17		Troops employed with their Bdes. on stables for horses, tracks, dugouts, bivouacs etc. Work on roads & craters existed on 27-4-17. Capt. Faquharson with 4 Sappers & 200 men of the Bde. commenced work on 28th on bring Road from ROEUVILLY - BEAUVRES.	
	30-4-17		Warm fine weather commenced on 28th, much improved	

[signature]
Major
OC 5 F.S. Squadron RE

TE RTRY

Army Form C. 2118.

WAR DIARY
or
INTELLIGENCE SUMMARY.
(Erase heading not required.)

5 -- F. L. Squadron R=
5 Can Div Vol 29

B.2 of 19??/7.

Place	Date	Hour	Summary of Events and Information	Remarks and references to Appendices
TERRY	1-5-17		Troops employed with their Bdes at constructing trui Nellies Morim trks Water Supply Bivouacs. Squadron was struck off unites as above on 1-5-17 for Squadron Training in Trek Training, Sat— Drills in the morning & Pl intro in afternoon. Capt Fergurson 3 saffeurs & average of 150 ORs inked morning Bedeaux from PROUILLY & BEAUVOIS, work completed on 13-5-17. The hours 13th B'ell 6" thick 7450 × 2" B'ell 3" thick 7300 × 3" B'ell 6" thick 1300 × at Mathewson 8 saffeurs & 450 average Drivers & Gunm Reinforcements worked on long S. parties of BOIS D'HAZNON from 3-5-17 -- 13-5-17. Completed. 1st B'ell 1320 × 2" × 3" B'ell 1500 handed on to CET Expeditionary Can Cav Bde took over sector of front line from 35th Div on 9.31. Central -- River OMIGNON. Lt Lees & 'B' Troop here to bivouac near VADENCOURT trench with Can Bde — and on arriving here inspected trenches, splinter proofs to HQ.	R. R. R. R.
	13-5-17			
MONTIGNY Dump	14-5-17			
	15-5-17		HQ. W.S. & Capt J with Lt Guerked & A Troop to MONTIGNY Dump. Major Glenn to Div H.Q. Nokecourt. From Lt Mathewson & C Troop to JEAN COURT trench with SEC'BAO Bde who took over front line sector from a Bde 59th Div from L2NA- 931 Ctr.	

WAR DIARY or INTELLIGENCE SUMMARY

Army Form C. 2118.

5/72 Sqdn RE
5th Cav Div
Vol 29 May 1917 contd.

Place: MONCHY-au-BOIS

Date	Hour	Summary of Events and Information	Remarks and references to Appendices
15-5-17		Work commenced on wiring Outpost Line, trucks, Cruickton Posts in Centre Attack Line & Support, wiring Intermediate Line, Grand Puits Wood Defences.	✓
19-5-17		OC Takes command of whole sector N. of HAMEL, COURT-ROMIGNON. One Sqdn RE & 1 Flying occupy North sector to L 24 a. Working parties under RE Supervision (Daily av. 250 hrs) on Grand Puits Defences & 3 70 troops 20 before each Trench & Support & Wires & Pillbox The above 370 troops replaces their own Div which went into trees on our left relieving the Inf. Bde N of L 57 = Div. Inf Coy working parties increases to 500 daily. Army to Intermediate Line work. No 4 breaks 1 Po "Tunnelly" Coy RE which now employs neckening hills in Durham. Start 12 Inf Supports & MGs etc under my orders "Under our sector N. of L 28 a. 5, 4 GRAND PUITS FM to 2 Cav Div Inf & Infy parties (are)	✓
23-5-17			✓ ✓
28-5-17		Line held as follows SE-DAR Bde fm GRAND PUITS FM - RED HOUSE CANADIAN Bde RED HOUSE - ROMIGNON. 4th Cav Div S/walk 87th trench. Bde 6th South. B Troop with Canadian Bde, C Troop with SE BDS. HQ. 6A Troop MONT/SMY Dump, Lt. Lees & Jones & trees TERRY. OC 5/72 Sqd gns	✓

F.A. Collins Major RE
OC 5/72 Sqdn

Army Form C. 2118.

WAR DIARY
or
INTELLIGENCE SUMMARY

5-20 Sqdn RE
5th Cav. Div. Vol 30 June 1917

(Erase heading not required.)

Instructions regarding War Diaries and Intelligence Summaries are contained in F. S. Regs., Part II. and the Staff Manual respectively. Title pages will be prepared in manuscript.

Place	Date	Hour	Summary of Events and Information	Remarks and references to Appendices
Montigny Dump	1-6-17		H.Q. & A Troop MONTIGNY DUMP, daily average of 250 Dismtd. Reinforcements of Reserve Bde. billets at VENDELLES and in LEVERGUIER Defences & wiring bel. same + valleys to East of it. 'C' Troop with 3rd/4th Bde billets at JEANCOURT and in Bde. sector. 'B' Troop with CANADIAN " VADENCOURT " " 100 men of Car. Reinforcements under Lt. Steward R.E. 180th T. Coy R.E. work in cmts. m Defences + East 180th T. Coy R.E. & 180th T. Coy R.E. work in party of 50 per Bde in line at work on dugouts in Intermed. line. Major COLLIN i/c ad Div.nl H.P. acting G.P.O. 5th Cav Div.	
	8.6.17		'B' & A Tps relieve each other in relief of Bdes.	¼
	15.6.17		'B' & C Troops " " " " "	¼
	21.6.17		All R.E. labour & working parties concentrate on work on Intermediate Line Support & on LEVERGUIER Defences	"
	30-6-17		100 extra men joined Dis.mtd. Reinforcements at VENDELLES for work in LEVERGUIER Defences	¼

H.H. Allen
Major RE
OC 5th & 7th Squad RE

Army Form C. 2118.

WAR DIARY or INTELLIGENCE SUMMARY.

(Erase heading not required.)

5th F. Squad. R.E.
5th Cav. Div. Vol 31 July 1917

Place	Date	Hour	Summary of Events and Information	Remarks and references to Appendices
MONTIGNY DUMP	1-7-17		H.Q. & A. Troop MONTIGNY Dump. Men working party 25th Dismtd. Regt working party. B. Troop with Canadian Cav. Bde billets at VRAINCOURT. "C" Troop with 5th Inf. Bde billets at VRAINCOURT.	
	9-7-17		Handed over KOKE 34 DWR + Oc. 20/ 7th Cav. Rgt. had one officer see maps. 2.3 miles wire entanglements as 7 × thick bunkers all intacts. Dug 8 new concentration points (dryland) put the stops. stops. shelling tranch boards to intersec. into dams + stops. Dug 37 rifle + bombers cells one support line. Dug to 3' deep. 4 keeps in LEVERGUIER with 1 foot 6 1/2 of Revetting, Cov with 30 hours Dugout + 4 callous north, practically finishes. 4 shelter pitted or Adv. Dressing station, took in R.a.M.C. Camouflage, Dug. Well 5.40 Deep. "Hogmes" Kitchen Refilling	"/"
TERTRY	10-7-17		R.M.L. Squadron encountries with horses in back billets at TERTRY. Refitting, cleaning up. etc. Capt. Farquharson to hospital on 9-7-17.	"/"
	13-7-17		Dismounted parade for G.O.C.S. inspection. Horses inspects + found fit. Capt. FARQUHARSON to hospital 9-7-17.	"/"
BUIRE	14-7-17		Squadron marched at 2 p.m. arrived at 5 p.m.	"/"
SUZANNE	15-7-17		" at 6 a.m. " 11 a.m.	"/"
RIBEMONT	16-7-17		" at 7 a.m. " 12 noon	"/"
MARIEUX	17-7-17		" at 7 a.m. " 1 p.m.	"/"
LATHIEULOYE	18-7-17		" at 7 a.m. " 3.30 p.m.	"/"

Army Form C. 2118.

WAR DIARY
or
INTELLIGENCE SUMMARY.

(Erase heading not required.)

5th FD Squad. RE.
3rd Cav. Div. (Vol. 31 Cont.) July, 1917.

Place	Date	Hour	Summary of Events and Information	Remarks and references to Appendices
LATHIEULOYE	19.7.17		Nil	
TROISVAUX	20.7.17		Marched at 3.30 pm arrd at 5pm Change due to lack of water at LATHIEULOYE	
"	↓		2 little G Troops employed on laying trestles over the hedges near HERNICOURT on R. TERNOISE and on musketry rifle practice near TROISVAUX.	
"	31-7-17			

F. W. Usher
Major RE.
OC. 5th FD Squad RE.

Army Form C. 2118.

3rd Field Squadron R.E.
5th Cav. Div? (Vol. 32) August 1917

WAR DIARY
or
INTELLIGENCE SUMMARY.
(Erase heading not required.)

Place	Date	Hour	Summary of Events and Information	Remarks and references to Appendices
TROISVAUX	1-8-17		Squadron in billets, horses on picket lines. Men employed during the month in training, inclising Musketry, Drill, Bridging, Equitation. Leave largely increased for men, only 3 men on 18 months in the country on 31-8-17.	
	31-8-17		Capt Farquharson returned from hospital on 26-8-17	

H.W.Weir
Major R.E.
O.C. 3rd Field Squadron R.E.

Serial No: 13
Army Form C. 2118.

5th Field Squadron R.E.
5th Cav. Div. Vol 33 Sept 1917

WAR DIARY
or
INTELLIGENCE SUMMARY.
(Erase heading not required.)

Instructions regarding War Diaries and Intelligence Summaries are contained in F. S. Regs., Part II and the Staff Manual respectively. Title pages will be prepared in manuscript.

Place	Date	Hour	Summary of Events and Information	Remarks and references to Appendices
TROISVAUX	1-9-17		Squad in billets. Horses in picket lines. Men employed in training chiefly Equitation, Musketry, gas helmet practice etc.	
	11-9-17		2nd Lt J. Kerr R.E. transferred on 10-9-17 to 7th Pontoon Park R.E.	
	12-9-17		An average of 1 Officer & 10 men employed daily in constructing a Drying Room for XVII Corps Laundry at ST MICHEL	
	14-9-17		Lt M. Babington rejoined the Squadron from 120th Ry Coy R.E.	
	16-9-17		Lt M. Babington & 25 O.R. Sappers proceeding daily from the [?] w.P.P.[?]	
			to work on huts in the new winter area	
	20.9.17		Capt. J. A. Daughworth leave proceeding to France	
	27.9.17		Major J.S. Collin " " "	
	29.9.17		Capt G.E. Franciere joined. Also Capt. Farquharson	
	30.9.17		Leave - 2 Officers and 47 men granted leave to UK	

C.E. Crunston Captain
5th [?]

Army Form C. 2118.

WAR DIARY
or
INTELLIGENCE SUMMARY.
(Erase heading not required.)

Instructions regarding War Diaries and Intelligence Summaries are contained in F. S. Regs., Part II and the Staff Manual respectively. Title pages will be prepared in manuscript.

Place	Date	Hour	Summary of Events and Information	Remarks and references to Appendices
TROIS VAUX	1.10.17		Squadron in billets – Normal routine	
	2.10.17		do.	
	3.10.17		1 Officer & 10 men on XVII Corps Laundry at Houdain	
	4.10.17		Squadron marches 1st F.M.D.R.S. at YVES — the rest of the march completed between squadrons and transport. Arrived & went into billets at BOURECQ.	
W. HOU	5.10.17		Gardens.	
	6.10.17		Squadron march to WATOU area – 3 squadrons in G.S.	
	7.10.17		3 Officers — 25 men – 3 Limbers advance party to WATOU prepared to billets.	
	13.10		Major C. G. WOOLNER R.E. assumed command of Squadron on transfer from 64th Field Company R.E.	
	14		Six lorries with party of Sappers collected jumping left in forward area by 13th Canadian Div.	
	15		do. All totals handed in to No. 3 W. Park ABEELE	
CAMPAGNE	16		Squadron marches with Cav. Bde. at 9.30 am CAMPAGNE A+B	
	17		Squadron marches with Cav. Bde. at 9 am. Billets for men & horses at BLENDECQUE	
RENTY			Arrives RENTY 3.35 pm.	
	20		Lt Chance + 10 Sappers attached Cav. Gas Helmet school at ST DENOEUX	A + B

Army Form C. 2118.

WAR DIARY
or
INTELLIGENCE SUMMARY.
(Erase heading not required.)

Place	Date	Hour	Summary of Events and Information	Remarks and references to Appendices
	21		Lt Greathead & 10 O.R. to REGNIER-ECLUSE dismantled huts	
	23		1 NCO. & 3 Sappers to Canadian Corps Equitation School at CAYEUX-SUR-MER.	
	24		Lt Chance on leave to U.K.	
	26		Lt Ray to relieve Lt Greathead.	
	27		Lt Greathead on leave to U.K. Part from REGNIER ECLUSE return. No trucks arrived so huts were dumped at HESDIN.	
	28		Lt Ray to 4th Field Sqdn H.Q. to relieve Lt Babington (leave) 3 tr.o.s to HESDIN to load huts	
	30		3 N.C.O.s returned; all huts loaded. Capt Grinsdale & Lt Matheson & 37 O.R. to go north with Can. Corps. 25 O.R. from 17 Bde Am. Col. R.H.A. to assist in grooms horses Squadron.	
	31		Part return from Can. Cav. Bde.	

11/4/17

Moodun Major R.E.
O.C. 5th Field Squadron R.E.

SECRET.   Copy No. 8

Appendix A

5TH CAVALRY DIVISION.

OPERATION ORDER NO. 38.

Ref. Map 1/100,000.   Dated 13th October, 1917.

1. The Division will march to an area South of MONTREUIL in accordance with attached March Table.

   Orders for the march from the BLEQUIN area to the MONTREUIL area will be issued later.

2. (a) Where Divisional Troops are shown as grouped with a Brigade they will march and billet under orders of that Brigade.

   (b) Divisional Headquarters and 5th Signal Squadron (less motors) will march under the orders of an officer to be detailed by the O.C., Signal Squadron.

   (c) Motor Ambulances and Sanitary Section will move under orders of A.D.M.S.

   (d) "B" Echelon will march with Brigades and Units of Divisional Troops.

3. A distance of 200 yards between Squadrons and groups of 10 transport vehicles is to be maintained.

4. Railhead October 14th - 15th at WIPPENHOEK.

   October 16th   at LUMBRES.

   October 17th   at HESDIN.

5. A Divisional Staff Officer will meet representatives from Ambala Brigade, Reserve Park, Ammunition Column and Signal Squadron at the E of LA CROSSE (1 mile North of RENESCURE) at 10 a.m. on 14th inst., and allot billets.

6. Divisional Report Centre will close at POPERINGHE at 11 a.m. on the 14th inst. and open at RENESCURE at the same hour.

7. ACKNOWLEDGE.

                                            H. T. Hodgson
                                            Lt-Colonel, G.S.

Issued by D.R. at 9-45 p.m.   5th Cavalry Division.

To/
   Normal O.O. Distribution Nos. 1 - 23.

   Second Army .... No. 25.
   Cavalry Corps .... No. 26.

5TH CAVALRY DIVISION.

March Table. (Issued with Operation Order No.38).

FORMATION OR UNIT.	STARTING POINT.	TIME.	ROUTE.	DESTINATION.	REMARKS.
Ambala Cav Bde. Mhow Field Ambulance. 17th Bde Ammn.Col. R.C.H.A. Ammn. Col.	Road Junction on ABEELE-STEENVOORDE Road ½ mile E. of STEENVOORDE Church.	9.30 a.m. Oct 14th.	STEENVOORDE - CASSEL.	RENESCURE Area.	Billets from Area Commandant, THIEMBRONNE.
---- do ----	ARQUES Church.	9 a.m. Oct 15th.	ARQUES - WIZERNES.	Southern portion of BLEQUIN Area.	
Signal Sqdn(less Motors) Divnl.Hqrs.(" ") Hqrs 17th Bde R.H.A.	K of HILLEHOEK.	11 a.m. Oct 14th.	STEENVOORDE - CASSEL.	RENESCURE AREA.	
---- do ----	ARQUES Church.	11 a.m. Oct 15th.	ARQUES - WIZERNES.	Southern portion of BLEQUIN Area.	Billets from Area Commandant, THIEMBRONNE.
Reserve Park.	K of HILLEHOEK.	11.15 a.m. Oct 14th.	STEENVOORDE-CASSEL	RENESCURE Area.	
---- do ----	ARQUES Church.	11.15 a.m. Oct 15th.	ARQUES - WIZERNES.	Southern portion of BLEQUIN Area.	Billets from Area Commandant, THIEMBRONNE.
Sec'bad Cav Bde. "N" Battery R.H.A. Sec'bad Field Ambulance.	Road Junction on ABEELE-STEENVOORDE Road ½ mile E. of STEENVOORDE Church.	10 a.m. Oct 15th.	STEENVOORDE - CASSEL.	RENESCURE Area.	Billets from Area Commandant, RENESCURE at ARQUES.
---- do ----	ARQUES Church.	9 a.m. Oct 16th.	ARQUES - WIZERNES.	Southern portion of BLEQUIN Area.	Billets from Area Commandant, THIEMBRONNE.
Canadian Cav Bde. Canadian Field Amb. R.C.H.A,Bde(less Am.Col) 5th Field Sqdn R.E. Hqrs A.H.T. Company.	Road Junction on ABEELE-STEENVOORDE Road ½ mile E. of STEENVOORDE Church.	10 a.m. Oct 16th.	STEENVOORDE -CASSEL.	RENESCURE Area.	Billets from Area Commandant,RENESCURE at ARQUES.

FORMATION OR UNIT.	STARTING POINT.	TIME.	ROUTE.	DESTINATION.	REMARKS.
Canadian Cav Bde. Canadian Field Amb. R.C.H.A.Bde(less Amn Col) 5th Field Sqdn R.E. Hqrs A.H.T.Company.	ARQUES Church.	9 a.m. Oct 17th.	ARQUES - WIZERNES.	Southern portion of BLEQUIN Area.	Billets from Area Commandant, THIEMBRONNE.
Motors of Divnl Hdqrs. No. 9 L.A.C. Battery.	POPERINGHE.	Oct 14th.	STEENVOORDE - CASSEL.	RENESCURE.	
---- do ----	RENESCURE.	Oct 15th.	ARQUES - WIZERNES.	THIEMBRONNE.	

Appendix B

SECRET. CANADIAN CAVALRY BRIGADE. Copy No. 19

OPERATION ORDER NO. 43.

Reference Maps
1/100,000   Dated October 15th, 1917

1. The Brigade, 5th Field Squadron and A.H.T.Coy., will march to an area South of MONTREUIL in accordance with the attached March Table.

   Orders for the march from the BLEQUIN Area will be issued later.

2. "B" Echelon will remain Brigaded under Lieut BONNICK and will be rationed separately.

   Number of men and horses to be reported by 6 p.m. 15th instant.

3. A distance of 300 yards between Squadrons and groups of ten transport vehicles is to be maintained.

4. Railhead October 15th.   WIPPENHOEK.
                16th.   LUMBRES.
                17th.   HESDIN.

5. All tents and Trench covers are to be left in situ, except those brought by units.

6. (a) Returned leave details that cannot be mounted will report at Brigade Headquarters and proceed in lorries with 2nd. blankets.
   (b) Lorries for 2nd blankets will be at Brigade Headquarters on afternoon of 15th instant.

7. Billeting Parties will proceed under orders to be issued by Staff Captain.

8. Brigade Report Centre closes at L.9.b.6.4. at 9 a.m. 16th inst., and will open at 2 p.m. at a point to be notified later.

9. ACKNOWLEDGE.

                                          Major,
                                     Brigade Major,
                              Canadian Cavalry Brigade.

Issued at 9 a.m. through Signals.

OPERATION ORDER DISTRIBUTION.

Copy No. 19, 5th Field Squadron.
  "   "   20 A.H.T. Company.

CANADIAN CAVALRY BRIGADE.

MARCH TABLE FOR OCTOBER 16th issued with OPERATION ORDER No.43.

Units in order of march.	Starting Point.	Time & Date.	Route to Starting Point.	Route to billets.	DESTINATION.	REMARKS.
Brigade H.Q. Signal Troop F.G.Horse. R.C.Dragoons L.S.Horse M.G.Squad'n. "A" Echelon R.C.H.A.Bde (less 1 (Colunm) "K" R.C.F.A. 5th Fld Sqn R.E. A.V.Section. "B" Echelon A.H.T.Coy.	Road junction on ABEELE - STEEN- VOORDE road ½ mile East of STEENVOORDE Church.	10.0 a.m. Oct.16th.	Second class road to BEDIAVOURDE. HILLHOEK ABEELE.	STEENVOORDE CASSEL.	REMESCURE Area.	Units will reconnoitre route to Starting point. "A" Echelon will rendez- vous on the STEENVOORDE - ABEELE road. Head of junction BEDIAVOURDE at 10.30 a.m. under Lieut. BENNETT. F.G.H. "B" Echelon under E.T.O., will rendezvous at the Eastern exit of ABEELE at 11.0 a.m. They will be billetted separately on route.

CANADIAN CAVALRY BRIGADE.

MARCH TABLE FOR OCTOBER 17th issued with OPERATION ORDER No.43.

Units in order of march.	Starting Point.	Time.	ROUTE.	DESTINATION.	REMARKS.
Brigade H.Q. Signal Troop L.S.Horse. F.G.Horse. R.C.Dragoons. E.G.Squad'n. "A" Echelon. R.C.H.A.Bde (less Amm.Col) 5th C.C.F.A. 5th Fld.Sqd'n R.E. R.V.Section. "B" Echelon. A.H.T.Coy.	ARQUES Church.	9.0 a.m. Oct. 17th.	ARQUES. VIZERNES.	Southern portion of B - E Q U I N Area.	"A" Echelon will follow Units to starting Point and proceed under Lieut. EMMETT. F.G.H.

Army Form C. 2118.

3 Field Squadron R.E.
November 1917

WAR DIARY
or
INTELLIGENCE SUMMARY.
(Erase heading not required.)

Instructions regarding War Diaries and Intelligence Summaries are contained in F.S. Regs., Part II. and the Staff Manual respectively. Title pages will be prepared in manuscript.

Place	Date	Hour	Summary of Events and Information	Remarks and references to Appendices
RENTY	2		G.O.C. inspected horses at 11.0 a.m.	
	4		One Sapper to each Brigade to assist in erection of huts.	
	7		Water troughs arrive; erection started. Lt Greatheed & Lt Chown from leave	
	8		14 O.R. rejoined from 3rd Fd Squadn. to assist in march.	
LEBIEZ	9	10 am	Marched to LEBIEZ.	
REMAISNIL	to	7.15 am	Marched to REMAISNIL. 15 O.R. R.H.A. joined Divl. Distlict. at WAVRIN. Appdx. B, C	Appendix B, C
LAHUSSOYE	11	8.0 am	Marched to LA HUSSOYE. Spr Mair accidentally killed by motor car. Appendix D	Appendix D
			Detachment under Lt Matheson transferred from 3rd F.S. to 2nd F.S.	Appendix E
			O.C. to Divl. H.Q.	
CAPPY	12	4 pm	Marched to CAPPY. Lt Bethune on leave joins Detachment with 2nd F.S.	Appendix G
FAY'S WOOD	13	4 pm	Marched to FAY'S WOOD to join 8 of 2nd F.S. Y.M.C.A. van detachment (less Lieut Appdx. H	Appendix H
			6 men with Capt. Grimsdale at NORTH) rejoined. Ry detachment rejoins	
			from 4 F.S.	Appendix J
	14		O.C. rejoined from Divl. H.Q. Wrote on leaving to Role address O.C. troops	
			Lt Greatheed to exchange with Capt. Grimsdale & proceeded to DESSART	Appendix K
			WOOD + ÉTINS. Lt Chown to BOUZY to assist in hutting Canadian Bde.	

WAR DIARY or INTELLIGENCE SUMMARY.

(Erase heading not required.)

Army Form C. 2118.

Place	Date	Hour	Summary of Events and Information	Remarks and references to Appendices
BIAS WOOD	18		Detachments on patrol rejoined Squadron.	
	19		B Troop with L.G.S. joined Canadian Bde. C Troop joined Sec'nd Bde.	
	20		H.Q. & A Troop marches at 1.45 am to join Antwala Bde Group, proceeding to concentration area DESSART WOOD. A Echelon marches at 2.15 am to TINCOURT. Joined Div¹ A₃ Echelon then marches to DESSART WOOD. B Echelon marches at 2.15 pm. to BOUCLY to Div¹ B Echelon. It (?) breathed joined A Troop at DESSART WOOD; was on water supply fatigue to B Echelon at BOUCLY. Watered twice in concentration area. Moved off with Antwala Bde at about 12.30 pm. Halted behind Sec'nd Bde at a point midway between VILLERS FAUCON + MARCOING. O.C. formed to reconnoitre situation in MARCOING. Infantry situation. Squadron bivouaced with Antwala Bde.	Appendices L, M, N
	21		A Troop with Antwala Bde. to 1st Cav. Div. Sq. H.Q. to Div¹ H.Q. Group Bivouaced in Hindenburg Line. C Troop made water point in VILLERS PLUICH which was not used owing to move of Div.	
	22		Squadron concentrated at EQUANCOURT.	
	23		Marched to SUZANNE.	Appendix O.

Army Form C. 2118.

WAR DIARY
or
INTELLIGENCE SUMMARY.
(Erase heading not required.)

Instructions regarding War Diaries and Intelligence Summaries are contained in F. S. Regs., Part II. and the Staff Manual respectively. Title pages will be prepared in manuscript.

Place	Date	Hour	Summary of Events and Information	Remarks and references to Appendices
SUZANNE	24		On 40 minutes notice.	Appendix P
VAUX	25		Marched to hutted billets in VAUX. 40 min. notice cancelled. B Echelon rejoined.	Appendix Q
	27		Marched to winter billets near TREFCON.	Appen. R, S
TREFCON	28		All Officers taken stock of hutting situation in winter area. Much material scattered + being wasted. Capt. Grimsdale + 2nd Lt. Matthewson on leave.	
	29		Orders received re taking over hand. from 24th Div. Troops on hutting in Bde area. 23 lorry-loads of hutting material arrive. O.C., 16 Grenadiers, & 2nd Lay round the line with O.C. 104th Fd. Co. R.E. While the van area the Division was just on ½ hr. notice to move. By chance was the only Officer in camp. Many new arrive scattered over the Divisional area or worked. Troops + A 3 Echelon moved off at 11.15. am + took up correct place in column (Animo Sec'tion Bde). O.C. whole Div HQ (next EPEHY).	Appen. T, V, V
	30		No knowledge at H.Q. of whereabouts of Squadron. It breathed found Squadron & brought it to Div H.Q.	Appendix W

16/3/17

A Mortimer Major RE
O.C. 5th Fd. Sqdn. R.E.

WAR DIARY or INTELLIGENCE SUMMARY

Army Form C. 2118.

9th Field Squadron RE

December 1917

Page 23.

Place	Date	Hour	Summary of Events and Information	Remarks and references to Appendices
JACQUENNE COPSE	1		C Troop to Secundrabad Pde for consolidation. B Troop to Canadian Pde. Little useful work done. B Whelon moved to ATHIES	Appen A.B. & D
	2		OC & 1st Breathes round the line 8.0 am. Division relieves from the line. Squadron at disposal of C.I.D Cav. Corps. A & B Troops assisting 1st F.S. with strong point (K.18.d). OC. 1st Guards Brigade troops from A&B Troops with 200 Cavalry now Second line.	Appen E Appen F
REUDICOURT	3		A Troop arriv. in front of VAUCHELETTE FARM. Squadron moved to Sentecom road & out of HEUDICOURT (dugouts). L. Babington from leave.	Appen G.H
	4		B Troop arriv. Bosson line north Cavalry pats. C Troop on strong point (K.18.d) with Cavalry works parts.	
	5		B Echelon rejoined. No work.	
	6		Squadron marches to VILLERS FAUCON (tents)	
VILLERS FAUCON CAULAINCOURT	11		Squadron marched to CAULAINCOURT. Billeted Hut No 206. Regiment of French Field Artry. A Troop completes at HERVILLY. Squadron at disposal of C.I.D Cav Corps. 2 Work parties each 150 dismounted men & 3 G.S. wagons to HERVILLY & POEUILLY refreshing.	Appen J.K Appen L.M
	12		A Troop on switch from FERVACQUE FARM to HESBÉCOURT (A Smith)	

WAR DIARY or INTELLIGENCE SUMMARY.

(Erase heading not required.)

Army Form C. 2118.

Place	Date	Hour	Summary of Events and Information	Remarks and references to Appendices
CROUNCOURT	13		A patrol rushed into ens. trs. Gauthier.	
	14		Negotiated for New A patrol of Ampotato Crowd from Hamill. York Stables.	
			according to C/Sergt.	
	16		Division 4th Reinforcements returning from ATHIES	
TREFCON	17		Supply column with 1200 cart of TREFCON. Division returns to winter area.	
	19		5 more L.G.S. wagon attached at HERVILLY	
	22		B patrol from PERVACOUE FARM to JEANCOURT billeted with ens.	
	23		C patrol from LE VERGUIER to BELLECOURT billets with ens. & tr Cay. ATTACK	
			relieved by A patrol at HERVILLY	
	24		D patrol marched out with tr Chance. C patrol marches out & men go chants	
			with cavalry pickets to the job.	
	25		Christmas Day. No work. The men were given an £1 Christmas dinner and supplies bought in Amiens +E.F.C. Two pigs amongs other things had been bought.	
			A piano was hired from NESLE	
	26		B transport 250 men 2nd Durn. Light worked on C patrol. 3 men L.G.S. HERVILLY for the week.	

Army Form C. 2118.

WAR DIARY
or
INTELLIGENCE SUMMARY.
(Erase heading not required.)

Place	Date	Hour	Summary of Events and Information	Remarks and references to Appendices
TREFCON	28		Troop with 400 Cavalry shades work on C Switch. 10 men of C troop to live at JEANCOURT. Capt FABAN came to Div. HQ on DADMS. 8 more LGS wagons reported daily at BIHECOURT for carrying pickets.	
	30		Capt Grimsdale to R.E. School BLENDECQUES. Defence of JEANCOURT & CARPEZA before sites with C.R.E. & Lt-Col—	

11·11·8

Morlen
Major NS
O.C. 5th Field Squadron NZ

O.C. 5th Field Squadron R.E.   Appendix A
                                T. X. 11. 17.

I am going to wire tonight from
X.2.c.2.8. to X.8.a.3.9.
approx. I am taking my limbers
out wire & pickets to SAUCHIE
WOOD if possible. I shall
be in front of POONA HORSE.
Can you send wire & pickets
to a point near here. You
can reply to this at R.E. dump
HEUDECOURT. W.17.c.2.2. I
will have a man there. K Hay, Lt, RE

8.30 P.M.   P.T.O.

I have dumped contents of
limbers with my horses at old
Bde. H.Q.   W.28.

K.R.

"A" Form
MESSAGES AND SIGNALS.

Army Form C. 2121 (In pads of 100.)

Appendix B

TO: 5th Fld Squadron

Sender's Number: M7A
Day of Month: 1

Send a Field Troop to H.Q. Canadian Cav Bde W.18.d. for work to-night on consolidation & wiring etc.

From: 1st Cav Div
Time: 8.10 pm

J.J. Hodgson

Appendix C

Dr Ray,
    Your note received.
Another troop has been ordered to report to Can. Bde. It Chance has been sent there with two G.S. waggons & one of pickets.
He will take the right half of the Divisional sector & you will take the left half. Carry on with small posts as I instructed you; Chance will do the same. They will return here at dawn; you will take your orders from G.O.C. See back Rd.
I cannot send you any more wire; if you want more you must fetch it from HEUSKOORT dump in your L.G.S.
Rations are being sent to you too.
    1/24/17 9.30 p.m.   A.N. Woodrum

"A" Form
MESSAGES AND SIGNALS.   Army Form C. 2121

Appendix D

TO { Lahore Bde
      Ambala Bde
      Canadian Bde   GOC & CRE
                        & CRA

Sender's Number: GS 884   Day of Month: 2   AAA

Strong hostile attack is expected this morning aaa the Bde will hold the front it now occupies at all costs aaa Ambala Bde will hold in readiness remainder of 11th Bn 6 Dgns in readiness to support Lee but at short notice aaa One officer 8th Hussars will report to GOC Lahore Bde remain at his HQrs ready to carry orders to the Regt aaa Every effort will be made by troops above named to strengthen position by wiring etc. Acknowledge

From 5th Cav Divn
Place
Time 12.10 pm

"A" Form
MESSAGES AND SIGNALS.

Army Form C. 2121
(in pads of 100)

Priority

This message is on a/c of: Appendix E

TO: 5th Field Squadron O.C. A.S.C.
Ambala Bde
P.

Sender's Number: GA.698
Day of Month: 3
AAA

Ref GA 697 of 2nd. AAA
The 5th Field Squadron will remain in
it's present position and not move
to Area in square E.23 as ordered. AAA
The 5th Fld Squadron will be under the
C.R.E. Cav Bde until further advice. AAA
Address 5th Fld Squadron repeated O.C. A.S.C.,
Ambala Bde & P.

From: 5th Cav Bde
Time: 9 AM

M.P. Hodgson Lt Col

Appendix F.

C.R.E. Cav. Corps.

    Work Report for night of 2nd/3rd.

2 Troops assisting 4th F.S. in digging & wiring strong point (W.18.d)

200 cavalry + 10 L.G.S. wagons wiring new Second Line from W.12.d.5.0 to W.5.d.cent. One line of French wire throughout and an apron for about half the distance. Gaps of 5ft every 100x.

Gaps in trench line closed (by spitlocking only) from W.12.d.5.0 to about W.12.a.7.0.

1st F.S. persisted in laying a second belt of wire within ours at about W.12.a.3.3.

              J. Woodham
              Major NZ
          O.C. 5th Fd. Sqdn NZ

MESSAGES A...

Office of Origin and Service Instructions: Appendix G

TO: 5th Field Squadron

Sender's Number: EX 18
Day of Month: 3rd
AAA

Tonight's work complete strong point W18d71 and improve wire on old reserve line from front of strong point to right of working party 1st Cav Div about W11d93 AAA new line in front of reserve line not to be worked on AAA 20 wagons each Box dump 5 pm AAA DM at W16c at your disposal AAA work with 4 FS

From: CRE Cav Corps
Time: 4 pm

Appendix H

CRE. Cav. Corps.

Before receiving your EX18 last night I had been across to see Major Hill.

We arranged that he should complete the strong point himself & that I should go on with the Reserve Line.

As I did not require all my Sappers for this we agreed that I could rest two of my Troops which had been out every night with Brigades of 5th Cav. Divn.

I sent out one Troop with 2 RE Officers and a working party of 200 to wire the old Reserve Line from W18 d 6.6 to V11 d 9.3

The wagons you detailed for me had orders to report to 4th F.S. Major Hill, however did not require them & told my Officer he could have them.

4th F.S. were working on the
Reserve line wire between
W18d.6.6 & W11d.9.3 & the
strong point so that my party
was superfluous.
It was agreed that they should
therefore wire the front line in
front of WAUCHELETTE FARM,
where the O.C. Infantry on the
spot said the wire was very
weak.

Wire as in rough
sketch was erected
from W18d.0.0 to
junction with 1st F.S.
at about W18c.5.8
(length about 500x); some of it
has additional French wire under
the aprons.

X Section

4/10/17

C.Woolmer
Major RE
O.C. 5th Fld. Sqdn RE

"A" Form.
MESSAGES AND SIGNALS.

Army Form C. 2121.
(In pads of 100.)

No. of Message..............

Prefix....Code....m	Words.	Charge.	This message is on a/c of:	Recd. at....m
Office of Origin and Service Instructions.				Date
VAR	Sent At....m To....		...................Service.	From
	By	(Signature of "Franking Officer.")		By

TO { 5th Field Sqdn VIth HQ ?
     Ambulance Cav Bde ? HQ

Sender's Number.	Day of Month.	In reply to Number.	A A A
GA 800	15		

5th Field Sqdn on relief from line to E.29.3 SE of VILLERS FAUCON where bivouac will be allotted them by BM ? Ambulance Cav Bde ? ? 5th Field Sqdn

From
Place: 5 Cav Div
Time: 7.50 ?

The above may be forwarded as now corrected. (Z)

.... Censor. Signature of Addressee or person authorised to telegraph in his name.

* This line should be erased if not required.

"A" Form.
MESSAGES AND SIGNALS.

Army Form C. 2121.
(In pads of 100.)

No. of Message............

Prefix	Code	Words	Charge	This message is on a/c of:	Recd. at....m.
Office of Origin and Service Instructions. *Appendix K*		Sent At....m. To.... By....		..........Service. (Sig. of "Franking Officer.")	Date.... From.... By....

TO { 5th Field Squadron

Sender's Number	Day of Month	In reply to Number	AAA
G25	6th		

You will move today to E.29 via SAULCOURT rejoining your division

From C in C Cav Corps
Place
Time

The above may be forwarded as now corrected. (Z)
....
Censor. Sig. of Addressor or person authorised to telegraph in his name.

* This line should be erased if not required.

"C" Form.
MESSAGES AND SIGNALS.

Army Form C. 2123.

TO: 5th Field Sqdn R.E. Via 24th Divn / O Cavdn Cav Bde

Sender's Number: LA 906
Day of Month: 10th

Your squadron will move to PŒUILLY (Peronne) aaa One should be located at troop to be located at HERVILLY aaa No accommodation exists either place so full tentage to be taken with you aaa addsd 5th Field Sqdn reptd 5th Cavy divn Cav Corps Cav Corps

FROM: CRE Cav Corps

"A" Form
MESSAGES AND SIGNALS.

TO: 5th Field Sq.

Sender's Number: Ga.915
Day of Month: 10/12

Cavalry Corps wire begins aaa 5th Field Sqdn will be placed at the disposal of CRE Cavalry Corps from 10th inst. aaa ends

From: 5th Cavalry Divn

5th Field Squadron RE Army Form C. 2118.

January 1918

WAR DIARY
INTELLIGENCE SUMMARY.
(Erase heading not required.)

Place	Date	Hour	Summary of Events and Information	Remarks and references to Appendices
TRE FCON	2		Two Sections 283 A.T. Coy R.E. joined for work on huts in Divisional Area and Corps huts.	
	4		Two troops on Corps Defences. A troop on Corps huts.	
	6		Lieut. Mackinnon returned from sick leave. Lieut. Maclean 7th D.G. attached to Squadron to assist in care of horses. All 3 officers being fully employed on works. Lieut. Fogg 283 A.T. Coy R.E. joined from base.	
	7		7 men A troop to JEANCOURT.	
	8		Lts. Gnathgro? & Mathewson with 10 men to JEANCOURT.	
	10		See appendix A (Mine Report)	Appendix A
	18		Lt. Fogg and one Section 283 A.T. Coy R.E. rejoined their Coy H.Q. at POEUILLY. Captain Hayzano 11th Hussars attached for work on Corps Defences.	
			now with O.C. 283 A.T. Coy R.E. at Barony.	
	20		Proceed to JEANCOURT. 6 D.G. Lt Mitchell and Lt Ritchie, Essex Yeo. attached JEANCOURT for work on defences	
	21		Remainder of 283 Coy R.E. rejoined their unit.	
	23		Working parties of 4th coy Can. Divr moved for the last time.	Appendix B
JEANCOURT	26		Squadron H.Q. moved to JEANCOURT on 8th Divn going into the line. Lt Maclean replaced by Lt Hinton 7 D.G.	

Army Form C. 2118.

WAR DIARY
INTELLIGENCE SUMMARY.
(Erase heading not required.)

Place	Date	Hour	Summary of Events and Information	Remarks and references to Appendices
JEANCOURT	27		Working parties of 2nd & 3rd Divs. worked for the last time. The remainder of the month there being no parties were devoted to getting materials together to carry out and make plans for the routine and proposed	
			1/2/18	
			Moughn Major ? O.C. 5th Fld Sqdn ?	

Appx A.

CAE Cav Corps

Progress Report for week ending 16/4/18

(a) New Trenches. 'A' Switch. S/putlocks complete (flat revetment deepening). Posts done to depth.
    'B' Switch. S/pitlocking complete.
    'C' Switch. S/pitlocking complete.

(b) Nil
(c) Nil
(d) Wire. 'A' Switch. complete.
    'B' Switch. complete.
    'C' Switch. complete.
    V.T.T Line. complete between 'B' Switch & JEANCOURT.
    Jeancourt defences. complete on E and S. sides.

(e) Nil
(f) Nil
(g) Miscellaneous. V.T.T Line marked out between 'A' & 'B' Switches.
    Bronx Line. Marking out & getting materials on site.

17/4/18
Moolman Major
O.C. 1st Fld Sqdn

Appendix B

S.197

4th Cav Corps

Progress Report for week ending 23.1.18

(c) New Trenches. 'A' Switch. Spitlocking complete. Posts dug to depth.
'B' Switch. Spitlocking complete. One post dug to depth.
'C' Switch. Spitlocking complete. All posts except two dug to depth.
V.J.T. Line. Spitlocked between 'B' Switch & JEANCOURT. Lot dug to depth.
Brown Line Support. Spitlocked from JEANCOURT to SMALL FOOT WOOD.

(d) Wire. 'A', 'B', and 'C' Switches complete.
V.J.T. Line. Complete (except 200x) between 'A' Switch and JEANCOURT.
JEANCOURT Defences. Complete on E. and S Sides.

(g) Miscellaneous. All Brown Line Support and V.J.T. Line sited.
Collection of materials for further work.

25/1/18

Woolley
O.C. 5th Fld Sqdn RE

WAR DIARY
INTELLIGENCE SUMMARY
(Erase heading not required.)

5th Field Squadron Feb. 1918

Army Form C. 2118.

Place	Date	Hour	Summary of Events and Information	Remarks and references to Appendices
JEANCOURT	1st		Squadron employed on Corps Defence works.	
	2nd		Capt. GRIMSDALE rejoined from French Army.	
	4th		Major WOOLNER & 2nd Lt. RAY to England on leave.	
	14th		Lt BABINGTON leave to Paris.	
			2nd Lt. WHEATLEY attached from 3rd Field Squadn.	
	15th		Lt. HAMILTON & Lt. S. ROBSON (vice STEVENSON &ts	
	15th		Lt GREATHEAD & Lt GRANCE leave to England.	
	20th		Major WOOLNER & 2nd Lt RAY rejoined from leave.	
			5 OR. exchanged to 3 OR. into 5th field squadron.	
	21st		Major WOOLNER left squadron to command 23 Field Coy.	
	23rd		7 OR exchanged to 7 OR. with 4 Field Squadn.	
	23rd		Lt BABINGTON rejoined from Paris.	
	24th		3 OR. exchanged with 23rd Field Squadn to 3 OR.	
	25th		3 OR. " " " "	
	26th		Lt GREATHEAD rejoined from leave & Lt RITCHIE Essex Yeo rejoined regiment.	
	28th		Lt BABINGTON transferred to 1st Field Squadron.	

Army Form C. 2118.

5th Field Squadron RE
Oct. 1918.

WAR DIARY or INTELLIGENCE SUMMARY.
(Erase heading not required.)

Place	Date	Hour	Summary of Events and Information	Remarks and references to Appendices
JEANCOURT	28th		Lt. MATHIESON leaves U.K.	
			5 Offrs. 160 O.Rs. where R.H.R. train hunt. Horses remained at TREFCON under Lt. HINKSON 2/Sq. during whole month.	

A.E. Erwin Capt
O.C. 5th Field Squadron

Army Form C.2118.

5th Field Squadron

March 1918

WAR DIARY
or
INTELLIGENCE SUMMARY.
(Erase heading not required.)

Place	Date	Hour	Summary of Events and Information	Remarks and references to Appendices
JEANCOURT	1st		Capt. H.T. KEANE A.A.M.C. joined squadron from Lucknow C.F.A.	R.A.W
	3rd		Capt. O'CONNOR R.A.M.C. transferred to 4th Cav. Div.	R.A.W
			Major E.T.R. BUCHANAN A.E. joined from 3rd Field Squadron to take over command of Squadron.	R.A.W
	6th		Capt. G.E. GRINSDALE R.E. left Squadron for duty with 3rd Field Squadron R.E.	R.A.W
	5th		Lt. N.A. CHANCE R.E. rejoined from leave to U.K.	R.A.W
			Squadron wagon lines moved from TERTRY to ATHIES.	R.A.W
	9th		Capt. H.T. KEANE A.A.M.C. granted fortnight's leave to U.K.	R.A.W
	11th		Capt. J.H. FAIRCLOUGH R.E. joined Squadron from 3rd Field Squadron and was left in charge of wagon lines at ATHIES.	R.A.W
	12th		Capt. F.J.M. WALLER R.E. joined Squadron from 1st Field Squadron & joined detachment on Corps Defences at JEANCOURT	R.A.W
	13th		Lts. H.M. GREATHEAD and N.A. CHANCE with 7.O.R. joined wagon lines at ATHIES from JEANCOURT.	R.A.W
			Lt. TINKSON 7 D.G's rejoined his regiment.	R.A.W

Army Form C. 2118.

WAR DIARY or INTELLIGENCE SUMMARY.

5ᵗʰ Field Squadron

March 1918

(Erase heading not required.)

Place	Date	Hour	Summary of Events and Information	Remarks and references to Appendices
ATHIES	15ᵗʰ		Major BUCHANAN, Capt. WALLER, Lt. RAY, 3 Cavalry Officers and remainder of detachments at HERVILLY and TEMPICOURT joined wagon lines at ATHIES.	R.A.W
BURE	16ᵗʰ		Squadron moved from ATHIES to BURE (Huts). 3 Cavalry Officers attached for Corps defences rejoined their regiments.	R.A.W R.A.W
"	18ᵗʰ		Lt. G. G. MATTHEWSON R.E. rejoined from leave to U.K.	R.A.W R.A.W
"	19ᵗʰ		Major BUCHANAN, Capt. WALLER, Lt. CHANCE, Lt. RAY and 28 O.R. went on detachment from BURE to POEUILLY for work on Corps Defences (Tents).	R.A.W R.A.W
"	20ᵗʰ		Detachment at POEUILLY worked on redoubts in Corps defences	R.A.W R.A.W
DOINGT	21ˢᵗ		Detachment at POEUILLY rejoined Squadron at BURE. I.O.R. wounded at TEMPICOURT on detachment with R.A.A. Squadron left BURE for DOINGT (Huts).	R.A.W R.A.W
BARLEUX	22ⁿᵈ		Squadron left DOINGT for BARLEUX (Bivouacs)	R.A.W R.A.W
FOUCAUCOURT	23ʳᵈ		Squadron left BARLEUX for FOUCAUCOURT (Bivouacs)	R.A.W R.A.W

WAR DIARY or **INTELLIGENCE SUMMARY.**
(Erase heading not required.)

Army Form C. 2118.

5th Field Squadron
March 1918

Place	Date	Hour	Summary of Events and Information	Remarks and references to Appendices
CAIX	24th		Work on water point at ESTRÉES-DÉNÉCOURT carried out. Squadron left FOUCAUCOURT for CAIX (bivouacs). Troops stampeded past Squadron camp in night owing to German spy removing of Cavalry broken through; Squadron took up defensive line in front of GUILLAUCOURT until scare washed out.	Petn. Pstn. Pstn.
BAYONVILLERS	25th		Squadron left CAIX for BAYONVILLERS. 1st Battalion XIX Corps R.E. joined with Major BUCHANAN in command Capt. FAIRTLOUGH as adjutant, Lt. RAY as quartermaster.	
	26th		1st Battalion R.E. took over line; Major BUCHANAN, Capt. FAIRTLOUGH, Lt. RAY at Battalion hqs. at ROSIÈRES. Capt. WALLER, Lt. GREATHEAD, Lt. MATHEWSON, Lt. CHANCE and 70 O.R. in front line at ROUVROY. Squadron transport under S.S.M. moved to WARVILLERS, then to BEAUCOURT, then to DENUIN. 1 O.R. killed at ROUVROY.	Pstn.
	27th		Battalion Hqs. moved to CAYEUX & then to DENUIN.	

Army Form C. 2118.

WAR DIARY
or
INTELLIGENCE SUMMARY.
(Erase heading not required.)

5th Field Squadron
March 1918

Instructions regarding War Diaries and Intelligence Summaries are contained in F. S. Regs, Part II. and the Staff Manual respectively. Title pages will be prepared in manuscript.

Place	Date	Hour	Summary of Events and Information	Remarks and references to Appendices
	27th (contd.)		Trench party in action at ROUVROY and at WARVILLERS. Lt. G.G. MATHEWSON killed, Lt. H.M. GREATHEAD wounded; 2 O.R. killed, 4 O.R. wounded, H.O.R. missing, 2 O.R. wounded and remaining at duty.	See Appendix "A"
				R&W
BOVES	28th		Trench party marched back & rejoined at DEMUIN. Squadron with transport less Battalion Hqs left DEMUIN for BOVES (billets).	R&W
"	29th		Battalion Hqs. still at DEMUIN; Squadron resting.	R&W
CAMBOS FM.	30th		Major E.T.R. BUCHANAN wounded, Lt. H.M. GREATHEAD wounded, on 27th evacuated. Battalion in action at DEMUIN under Capt. FAIRTLOUGH. Squadron left BOVES for CAMBOS FARM (billets).	R&W
"	31st		Capt. FAIRTLOUGH with details of squadron rejoined at CAMBOS FARM. Battalion disbanded. 1 Officer 39 O.R on leave during month.	R&W

(M. Wralen)
Capt. V. R.E.

Appendix A

On arrival at ROUVROY on morning of of 26th they found the infantry retiring and immediately took up an outpost line on the East of the village. Roads were blocked and the position consolidated and held as outposts until the infantry came up in the afternoon and filled in the flanks; these infantry came under command of the Field Squadron. During the night a motor car which approached the line was put out of action and the occupants killed. Early on the 27th, one officer prisoner was captured and about 11 a.m. the enemy attacked between VRELY and ROUVROY and the infantry on the left retired; about the same time the enemy broke the line by BOUCHOIR and the infantry on right also retired. The Squadron conformed with the retirement considerably harassing the enemy's advance and at one period being able to use very effective rifle fire on close formations of the enemy at 100x range and a was taken up in front of WARVILLERS, from which the squadron was withdrawn about midnight

WAR DIARY
or
INTELLIGENCE SUMMARY.
(Erase heading not required.)

Army Form C. 2118.

5th Field Squadron R.E.
April 1918

Place	Date	Hour	Summary of Events and Information	Remarks and references to Appendices
LAMOTTE-BREBIÈRE	April 1st		Squadron moved from CORBAS FARM to the Sawmill East of LAMOTTE-BREBIÈRE (Huts). Came under Cavalry Corps again for administration and work.	DAW
"	1st-3rd		Squadron employed on two bridges over canal under C.R.E. Cav. Corps	DAW
"	4th		18 O.R. Reinforcements arrived from 4th Field Squadron R.E.	DAW
"	5th		Orders received that 5th Field Squadron was to be broken up and absorbed as reinforcements	DAW
AILLY-LE-HAUT-CLOCHER	9th		Squadron moved from LAMOTTE-BREBIÈRE to AILLY-LE-HAUT-CLOCHER (billets).	
			Captain G. H. FAIRLOUGH transferred to 3rd Field Squadron R.E.	
			Lt. N. A. CHAYCE transferred to 2nd Field Squadron R.E.	
			2 Lt. K. RAY transferred to 1st Field Squadron R.E.	
			Lt. A.B.S. EDWARDES (attached) returned to Cav. Corps Bridging Park.	DAW
			Interpreter COSTE transferred to French Mission H.Q. 1st Cav. Div.	
ROUEN	16th		Squadron less Captain F.T.H. WALKER and 7 O.R. proceeded to R.E. Base Depot.	DAW

Army Form C. 2118.

3rd Field Squadron RE
April 1918

WAR DIARY
or
INTELLIGENCE SUMMARY.
(Erase heading not required.)

Place	Date	Hour	Summary of Events and Information	Remarks and references to Appendices
ROUEN	16 (contd.)		Captain H.T. KEARNE R.A.M.C. transferred to 2nd Cav. Div. Handing over of all vehicles, animals, and stores completed	R.T.W
"	18		Captain F.J.A. WALLER and 7 O.R. proceeded to R.E. Base Depot.	R.T.W
"	20		Captain WALLER and 7 O.R. arrive R.E. Base Depot. Captain F.J.H. WALLER and all personnel 3rd Field Squadron R.E. transferred to R.E. Base Depot.	R.T.W

SECRET

Dels
3rd Echelon
Base

> 5TH
> FIELD SQUADRON, R.E.,
> 5TH CAVALRY DIVISION.
> No. FS/346
> Date. 22/4/18

War Diary of this Unit
for the Month of APRIL 1918
is forwarded herewith for your
disposal.

B H Walker
Captain RE
OC 5 Field Sqn RE

www.ingramcontent.com/pod-product-compliance
Lightning Source LLC
Chambersburg PA
CBHW081243170426
43191CB00034B/2025